GENDER DYSPHORIA

IS GENDER DYSPHORIA A MENTAL ISSUE AND WHAT

CAN BE THE SYMPTOMS

DR. MARK ROGERS

Table of Contents

CHAPTER ONE

INTRODUCTION

Gender dysphoria is the sensation of pain or distress that could get up in human beings whose gender identification differs from their sex assigned at beginning or intercourse-related physical traits.

Transgender and gender-diverse human beings may additionally revel in gender dysphoria in some unspecified time in the future in their lives. However, some transgender and gender-numerous human beings experience comfortable with their bodies, without or with medical intervention.

A prognosis for gender dysphoria is

protected within the Diagnostic and Statistical guide of intellectual problems (DSM-five), a guide posted by means of the yank Psychiatric association. The analysis was created to help human beings with gender dysphoria get get entry to to crucial health care and powerful remedy. The term makes a speciality of soreness due to the fact the problem, in place of identification.

Gender dysphoria occurs in those who are transgender (trans). It causes emotional misery due to differences among a person's gender identification and physical appearance. Many humans experience better after speakme with a therapist and exploring gender confirmation alternatives.

Gender dysphoria describes a experience of

unease regarding the mismatch amongst assigned gender and gender identity. This experience impacts many — however now not all — transgender humans in advance than they start living as their actual selves (transition and gender expression). And it may occur at any issue in the route of lifestyles, from adolescence to adulthood. People with gender dysphoria may additionally additionally experience extreme emotional and mental misery inside the event that they're not able to express their skilled gender and/or if they don't receive the guide and popularity they need.

Gender dysphoria is a scenario that causes misery and pain at the same time as the gender you grow to be aware of with conflicts with the intercourse which you had been assigned at shipping. You may have been assigned a male intercourse at beginning but feel which you're lady, or vice versa. Or you could trust your self to be neither intercourse, or a few component in between or fluid.

This disconnect amongst how society regards you and how you enjoy bodily and mentally can cause excessive misery, anxiety, and depression. Gender dysphoria turned into once called "gender identification sickness." however it's no longer a intellectual infection.

Gender dysphoria isn't the same as sexual orientation.

Gender dysphoria refers to emotions of misery and pain that someone critiques when their assigned gender does now not healthy their gender identity. Folks who enjoy gender dysphoria can also experience uncomfortable with and distressed over the warfare between the sexual tendencies of their physical frame and the manner they sense and consider themselves.

They will also revel in emotions of distress or pain over the conventional gender roles anticipated of their assigned gender.

The results of gender dysphoria can variety from one individual to the next. For some people, those emotions of battle may also have an impact on their self-picture and conduct. A person with gender dysphoria may additionally moreover cope with pain via altering their gender expression, gender illustration, or gender challenge from their gender assigned at start. They will additionally make modifications to their bodily look.

Kids who experience gender dysphoria may also moreover specific their desire to be the other gender and call for on toys, hairstyles, and clothing normally associated with the opposite gender.

Now not anyone who has gender dysphoria identifies as transgender, however many humans diagnosed with gender dysphoria do understand as transgender, gender fluid, or gender non-conforming.

Symptoms

Gender dysphoria would possibly reason

younger human beings and adults to enjoy a marked distinction among inner gender identification and assigned gender that lasts for at the least six months. The distinction is tested thru at the least of the subsequent:

A difference among gender identity and genitals or secondary sex tendencies, including breast length, voice and facial hair. In younger youth, a difference amongst gender identity and anticipated secondary sex traits.

A sturdy choice to be rid of those genitals or secondary sex traits, or a desire to prevent the improvement of secondary intercourse tendencies.

A strong desire to have the genitals and secondary intercourse trends of every other gender.

A strong choice to be or to be handled as any other gender.

A strong notion of getting the typical feelings and reactions of each other gender.

Gender dysphoria may purpose substantial distress that affects the way you characteristic in social situations, at artwork or university, and in different regions of lifestyles.

Gender dysphoria would possibly begin in formative years and maintain into adolescence and maturity. Or you'll possibly have durations in which you no longer enjoy gender dysphoria. You can also experience gender dysphoria across the time of puberty or tons later in life.

Gender nonconforming (GNC) is a sizeable term that includes human beings whose gender identification isn't strictly lady or male or movements among the two. Distinct phrases for this embody genderqueer, gender modern, gender impartial, bigender, noncisgender, nonbinary, and 1/3 sex.

People who enjoy gender dysphoria can also frequently explicit that they want to be the alternative gender. They regularly enjoy uncomfortable with the gender roles and gender expressions of their starting-assigned sex. This might take place in behaviors together with dressing as their desired gender, gambling with toys commonly associated with the alternative gender and rejecting many gender-stereotypical behaviors.

Gender dysphoria isn't always associated with an man or woman's sexual orientation. Those who enjoy gender dysphoria can be straight away, homosexual, lesbian, or bisexual. Folks who feel gender dysphoria will also be gender-nonconforming or transgender. However, it's miles essential to apprehend that no longer anyone who is transgender or gender nonconforming reports gender dysphoria.

What does it suggest to be transgender?

The term "transgender" is an umbrella term that describes humans whose gender identity and intercourse assigned at begin don't align primarily based on traditional expectancies of gender. As an instance:

Someone assigned woman sex at start (AFAB) whose gender identification is male.

Someone assigned male sex at beginning (AMAB) whose gender identity is woman.

The time period "transgender" can embody exclusive gender identities, too, and is evolving with new generations. Parents which can be transgender may be a combination of gender identities, or they will choose out as:

Nonbinary: someone who identifies as neither (or both) male or female.

Gender fluid: someone whose gender identity shifts back and forth.

Two-active: a native American, First countries or Alaska Natives man or woman who identifies as a 3rd gender who has a male spirit and woman spirit.

Individuals who're on the nonbinary spectrum may moreover further describe their gender identification with the aid of the usage of the use of descriptors together with "nonbinary transmasculine" or "nonbinary transfeminine," or also can use remarkable terminology which include "agender," "no-gender," "androgynous," and/or "gender queer."

CHAPTER TWO

Is gender dysphoria a mental contamination?

Gender dysphoria isn't a intellectual contamination. Rather, it describes the uneasiness stemming from the mismatch many of the experienced gender and assigned sex at shipping. However, a number of the unsightly emotions that once in a while accompany gender dysphoria consist of:

Tension.

Depression.

Consuming issues.

Put up-traumatic pressure disorder (PTSD).

Substance abuse.

Regardless of the fact that gender dysphoria isn't a highbrow contamination, whilst no longer addressed, it may bring about worsening mood troubles, despair and tension, and can in addition complicate the issues the people can be having. Coverage can also moreover cowl some illnesses related to gender dysphoria and gender dysphoria care.

What does gender dysphoria sense like?

Most people with gender dysphoria be bothered by way of extreme, complex feelings that stem from having the physical attributes of 1 gender and figuring out with both an opposite gender or a gender that doesn't wholesome the definition of binary genders (male and female).

You can enjoy:

Annoying.

Depressed.

Remoted.

Misunderstood.

Part of you is lacking.

Shameful.

Suicidal.

An urge to self-damage.

Uncomfortable together along with your appearance.

Gender dysphoria symptoms can start at any degree of existence.

What reasons gender dysphoria?

Researchers are though working to determine the reason. The condition might also begin with biological modifications that show up earlier than delivery.

The tension, stress and state-of-the-art soreness related to gender dysphoria may be associated with social stigma. Gender nonconforming children, kids and adults regularly face discrimination and verbal harassment. One in 4 are physical attacked, and extra than 1 in 10 are sufferers of sexual attack.

Prognosis of Gender Dysphoria

Gender dysphoria is listed in the Diagnostic and Statistical guide of highbrow problems (DSM-5). In the preceding version of the DSM, it was called gender identity disorder. This changed into changed in 2013 to eliminate the stigma related to calling it a sickness. Where it have become formerly supplied as a disorder related to identity, the DSM-5 takes a extra descriptive method this is centered on the discomfort and distress that dysphoria causes.

In younger humans and Adults

To be recognized with gender dysphoria as a youngster or character, an character want to revel in clinically massive distress or impairments in social, art work, and different vital lifestyles regions. The ones emotions must very last for at least six months and be followed through as a minimum of the following:

A big incongruence among number one and secondary intercourse trends and the character's professional gender

A marked desire to be rid of primary or secondary intercourse traits

A choice to have the number one or secondary intercourse trends in their skilled gender

A preference to be their experienced gender

A need to be treated as their skilled gender

A notion that they have got the behaviors, feelings, and reactions which may be traits of their skilled gender.

In kids

Youngsters also can revel in gender dysphoria. It isn't always uncommon for children to exhibit gender non-conforming behaviors. Consequently, it's vital to distinguish amongst general adolescence behaviors and genuine gender dysphoria.

Like adults, children want to experience impairments in functioning or splendid misery lasting as a minimum six months. They should also enjoy at the least six of the following signs and symptoms:

The insistence that they may be the

alternative gender or a choice to be the opportunity gender

A choice for engaging in fantasy play or make-bear in mind as the other gender function

A choice for garb usually related to the alternative gender

A choice for toys stereotypically preferred by way of the opposite gender

Rejecting toys or sports usually associated with their assigned gender

Expressing dislike for his or her bodily intercourse characteristics

A preference to have the intercourse developments that in shape their gender identity

Who prefer to play with extraordinary youngsters of the other gender

Signs and symptoms and symptoms of gender dysphoria in kids can be gift as early as age 4. Those symptoms often increase more immoderate as kids grow to be older, mainly once they experience the bodily adjustments related to puberty.

Remedy of Gender Dysphoria

Treatment for gender dysphoria is pretty person and based on everybody's unique wishes. It typically specializes in supporting the character explore their gender identification, regularly with the aid of allowing them to express their gender in a manner that corresponds to their inner experience of gender. This could embody dressing in a way that aligns with their gender identity, using particular names and pronouns, or taking scientific steps to alternate the frame physical.

Similarly to counseling, treatment for gender dysphoria can also include hormones and gender reassignment surgical treatment.

Medical options

Some humans with gender dysphoria may additionally select more huge treatment concerning gender-putting forward hormone treatment and gender-putting forward scientific processes. Remedy can also include frame changes that help align someone's outward presentation with their internal gender identification.

Hormone remedy and surgical procedure are ways to perform this. However again, treatment wishes to be adapted to the needs and desires of the individual. Some people may need to gain a complete transition to the gender with which they pick out. Others may also moreover want best to reduce the secondary sex trends, which includes facial hair or breasts, that don't align with their gender identification.

It's far critical to understand that whilst surgical gender confirmation surgical treatment is an option, no longer all people with gender dysphoria makes that preference. Surgical treatment is costly and commonly now not covered via manner of insurance, and not anybody desires to have complete gender reassignment. Hormone therapy may assist some humans, at the same time as others can also pick out to alternate their outward gender expression and get dressed to correspond with their inner enjoy of gender identification.

Masculinizing and feminizing hormones can on occasion assist lessen or solve emotions of gender dysphoria. Such hormones can have aspect outcomes, at the side of adjustments in libido and the potential for manic, hypomanic, or psychotic symptoms in human beings with an underlying psychiatric situation.

However, individuals who can't take any of these steps can also moreover begin to experience increased intellectual misery, inclusive of emotions of anxiety and depression. In such instances, psychotherapy may also additionally assist human beings experience extra at ease expressing their inner experience of gender and improve highbrow properly-being.

Psychotherapy

A few people can also desire to have counseling to assist them feel more comfortable with their emotions, affirm their identity, and help them cope or reduce any emotions of misery.

Courting or circle of relatives counseling can help partners, dad and mom, and other own family people higher apprehend what their loved one is experiencing. This will help the person gain social and peer manual, offering a greater maintaining environment.

Psychotherapeutic treatments for gender dysphoria do not try to change an person's gender identification. As an alternative, psychotherapy specializes in supporting human beings experience extra comfortable of their identity and expression of their gender.

The aim is to help human beings experience greater fulfilled and enhance their outstanding of life with the useful resource of lessening feelings of dysphoria. This is sometimes completed via:

Exploring gender identity and expression

Getting to know techniques to manage pressure

Practising self-reputation

Building a guide community

Making selections approximately transition options

Enhancing relationships

Therapy can help humans reduce feelings of dysphoria, but it may also help human beings at any phase of the machine enhance their high-quality of life and nicely-being.

CHAPTER THREE

Demanding situations

Parents that are gender nonconforming and their families are often at an multiplied chance of publicity to stigma and discrimination due to their gender identification. Human beings with gender dysphoria who are transgender or gender nonconforming even have a higher risk of being the sufferers of violence or bullying.

Folks that do pursue medical treatments which include hormones or surgical strategies can also face problems in gaining access to suitable healthcare and insurance coverage for their remedy.

Feelings of dysphoria blended with a lack of social guide can regularly contribute to highbrow distress and special troubles. Some issues associated with gender dysphoria encompass depression, tension, substance misuse, self-harm, and other highbrow health troubles.

Studies has additionally shown that humans with gender dysphoria have a better chance of lack of life thru suicide than the general population. One have a observe placed that 48.3% of participants with gender dysphoria had skilled suicidal ideation, and 23.Eight% had attempted suicide at the least as soon as.

Handling Gender Dysphoria

Managing feelings of gender dysphoria commonly entails remedy that specializes in supporting humans feel more comfortable with their gender identification. A few different strategies that would assist people control with emotions of gender dysphoria encompass:

Find assist: attempt turning into a member of a resource organization and speakme to pals who've had similar research.

Lessen soreness: utilize practices together with breast binding or genital tucking to lower bodily traits that make contributions to emotions of dysphoria.

Take care of yourself: Prioritizing self-care and emotional health, inclusive of doing subjects that make you experience suitable approximately your self and your frame.

Confirm your identity: attempt doing small matters in an effort to help confirm your gender identity. This may embody carrying fine accessories, changing your hairstyle, or asking others to consult you thru your selected pronouns.

Plan for the future: people may additionally moreover select to pursue criminal options to transition to their preferred gender and transition in social settings. Studies the stairs and make a plan to help you paintings within the path of your prolonged-term goals, whether or not the ones goals involve making a scientific, social, or crook transition.

Pronouns

A few human beings with gender dysphoria may favor to use pronouns similar to their gender identification. Or they may select the usage of the gender-unbiased, singular "they," "them," "their" pronouns.

As you work within the path of your lengthy-time period goals, look for answers which will also assist you deal with your emotions of dysphoria within the short term. This might include overlaying or minimizing your touch with the primary or secondary sex traits that reason emotions of distress. Spend time exploring your identification and the approaches of expressing it that revel in proper for you.

Crucial phrases to apprehend

Some key terms which might be related to gender dysphoria encompass:

Cisgender: Describes someone whose gender identity is aligned with the sex assigned to them at beginning

Gender expression: The strategies that humans outwardly explicit their gender identification, regularly thru their get dressed, physical look, mannerisms, and one of a kind traits

Gender identification: a person's inner sense and enjoy in their gender

Nonbinary: An umbrella time period to explain folks which are outdoor of the conventional male/woman gender binary

Transgender: An umbrella term to give an explanation for someone who diagnosed as a gender extremely good from the only they had been assigned at start

CONCLUSION

Emotions of gender dysphoria can also moreover come and move sooner or later of your lifestyles, but people residing with it may nevertheless have a extraordinary destiny. Treatment will let you gain self notion in expressing your preferred gender. You could choice to make small modifications at the beginning, like going by using the usage of a unique name. Everlasting modifications also can include scientific healing strategies and gender affirmation surgical treatment. The treatments which may be right for you and the tempo at that you pursue them are as plenty as you. An experienced healthcare company can help making a decision.

THE END

www.ingramcontent.com/pod-product-compliance
Lightning Source LLC
Chambersburg PA
CBHW060820260726

48660CB00003B/1019